Positivity Journal

Just

Breathe

One small positive thought in the morning
can change your day.

∞

Books With Soul
Somewhere in the desert, sea and forest.
www.bookswithsoul.com
∞
Books with Soul supports copyright for all authors.
Thank you for purchasing a copyrighted edition of this book.
First Edition 2018

one small positive thought
in the morning can change
your day
   -Dalia Lama

This positivity journal belongs to:

_____

Date: _____

Given by: _____

Congratulations!

You opened the book! Fantastic! Hopefully with pen in hand, YOU are ready to embark on an experiment.

It's okay if you're skeptical.
It's okay if you forget a day.
It's okay if the task seems impossible because you feel like your world is falling around you.

It's okay.

You opened the book, so at least TRY this experiment.

Put this book on your night stand, or beside your bed, tooth brush, or coffee maker. Leave it somewhere in the morning you can't help but see it.

Try this experiment for 21 days:

Every morning pause for five minutes and write a simple positive thought.

That's it!
Repeat it for 21 days and make a new habit.

It takes 21 days to make or break a habit.

Starting out with positivity every morning is certain to impact your day. Try it--see if it works. What do you have to lose?

Maybe no one will ever read your positive words--but you. And, in the future maybe you will stumble upon this book made of paper, because it can't be lost when the computer crashes, or when our fast-paced technology changes the way we share or store data. This journal is physical and will always be around.

Maybe one day you will jot down a great positive quote you heard that day, and it will inspire you or someone you love in the future.

Maybe it's simply noting the words of your heart, your goals or what you are thankful for.

A glance back at positive thoughts will only make your life more positive.

Try it, I dare you.

www.bookswithsoul.com

"You can't go back and change the beginning, but you can start where you are and change the ending."

-unknown

Positivity Journal

DAY 3

"I made my
bed this
morning."

Today's date: Fri, 1/25/19
My positive thought:

"Where ever you go,
there you are"

"It is the truth Ruth"

Today's date:
My positive thought:

Today's date:
My positive thought:

Positivity Journal

Today's date:
My positive thought:

Today's date:
My positive thought:

Today's date:
My positive thought:

It does not matter how slowly you go, just so you don't stop
-Confucius

Positivity Journal

Today's date:
My positive thought:

○————————————————————————○

Today's date:
My positive thought:

○————————————————————————○

Today's date:
My positive thought:

Positivity Journal

Today's date:
My positive thought:

○————————————————————————————○

Today's date:
My positive thought:

○————————————————————————————○

Today's date:
My positive thought:

The secret of getting ahead is getting started.

Positivity Journal

Today's date:
My positive thought:

⊖———————————————————————⊖

Today's date:
My positive thought:

⊖———————————————————————⊖

Today's date:
My postive thought:

Positivity Journal

Today's date:
My positive thought:

Today's date:
My positive thought:

Today's date:
My positive thought:

Live, Laugh, Love
Why not? Do you
know of a better
way to live?

Positivity Journal

Today's date:
My positive thought:

○————————————————————————————○

Today's date:
My positive thought:

○————————————————————————————○

Today's date:
My positive thought:

Positivity Journal

Today's date:
My positive thought:

Today's date:
My positive thought:

Today's date:
My positive thought:

Dream big, work hard, stay focused and surround yourself with good people.

Positivity Journal

Today's date:
My positive thought:

Today's date:
My positive thought:

Today's date:
My positive thought:

Positivity Journal

Today's date:
My positive thought:

Today's date:
My positive thought:

Today's date:
My positive thought:

Every day is a fresh start.

Positivity Journal

Today's date:
My positive thought:

○─────────────────────────────────────○

Today's date:
My positive thought:

○─────────────────────────────────────○

Today's date:
My postive thought:

Positivity Journal

Today's date:
My positive thought:

Today's date:
My positive thought:

Today's date:
My positive thought:

Positivity Journal

Today's date:
My positive thought:

Today's date:
My positive thought:

Today's date:
My positive thought:

If you want to fly give up everything that weighs you down.

Positivity Journal

Today's date:
My positive thought:

○————————————————————————○

Today's date:
My positive thought:

○————————————————————————○

Today's date:
My positive thought:

Positivity Journal

Today's date:
My positive thought:

○─────────────────────────────────────○

Today's date:
My positive thought:

○─────────────────────────────────────○

Today's date:
My positive thought:

Positivity Journal

Today's date:
My positive thought:

○────────────────────────────────────○

Today's date:
My positive thought:

○────────────────────────────────────○

Today's date:
My positive thought:

The future belongs to those who believe in the beauty of their dreams- Eleanor Roosevelt

Positivity Journal

Today's date:
My positive thought:

Today's date:
My positive thought:

Today's date:
My positive thought:

Positivity Journal

Today's date:
My positive thought:

○──○

Today's date:
My positive thought:

○──○

Today's date:
My positive thought:

Positivity Journal

Today's date:
My positive thought:

○————————————————————————————————○

Today's date:
My positive thought:

○————————————————————————————————○

Today's date:
My positive thought:

Never a failure
always a lesson.

Positivity Journal

Today's date:
My positive thought:

○──○

Today's date:
My positive thought:

○──○

Today's date:
My positive thought:

Positivity Journal

Today's date:
My positive thought:

○————————————————————————————○

Today's date:
My positive thought:

○————————————————————————————○

Today's date:
My positive thought:

Positivity Journal

Today's date:
My positive thought:

○─────────────────────────────────────○

Today's date:
My positive thought:

○─────────────────────────────────────○

Today's date:
My positive thought:

Life is beautiful.

Positivity Journal

Today's date:
My positive thought:

○————————————————————○

Today's date:
My positive thought:

○————————————————————○

Today's date:
My positive thought:

Positivity Journal

Today's date:
My positive thought:

○────────────────────────────────○

Today's date:
My positive thought:

○────────────────────────────────○

Today's date:
My postive thought:

Positivity Journal

Today's date:
My positive thought:

○━━━━━━━━━━━━━━━━━━━━━○

Today's date:
My positive thought:

○━━━━━━━━━━━━━━━━━━━━━○

Today's date:
My positive thought:

Just don't give up trying to do what you really want to do, where there is love and inspiration, I don't think you can go wrong.
Ella Fitzgerald

Positivity Journal

Today's date:
My positive thought:

○───────────────────────────────────○

Today's date:
My positive thought:

○───────────────────────────────────○

Today's date:
My positive thought:

Positivity Journal

Today's date:
My positive thought:

○───────────────────────────────────○

Today's date:
My positive thought:

○───────────────────────────────────○

Today's date:
My positive thought:

Positivity Journal

Today's date:
My positive thought:

○──○

Today's date:
My positive thought:

○──○

Today's date:
My positive thought:

A smile is a crooked line that sets things straight- Phyllis Diller

Positivity Journal

Today's date:
My positive thought:

○————————————————————————————○

Today's date:
My positive thought:

○————————————————————————————○

Today's date:
My positive thought:

Positivity Journal

Today's date:
My positive thought:

○━━━━━━━━━━━━━━━━━━━━━━━━━━━○

Today's date:
My positive thought:

○━━━━━━━━━━━━━━━━━━━━━━━━━━━○

Today's date:
My positive thought:

Positivity Journal

Today's date:
My positive thought:

○━━━━━━━━━━━━━━━━━━━━━○

Today's date:
My positive thought:

○━━━━━━━━━━━━━━━━━━━━━○

Today's date:
My positive thought:

The life I live is created by the story I tell - Abraham Hicks

Positivity Journal

Today's date:
My positive thought:

○━━━━━━━━━━━━━━━━━━━━━━━━━━○

Today's date:
My positive thought:

○━━━━━━━━━━━━━━━━━━━━━━━━━━○

Today's date:
My positive thought:

Positivity Journal

Today's date:
My positive thought:

○————————————————————————————○

Today's date:
My positive thought:

○————————————————————————————○

Today's date:
My positive thought:

Positivity Journal

Today's date:
My positive thought:

○─────────────────────────────────○

Today's date:
My positive thought:

○─────────────────────────────────○

Today's date:
My postive thought:

It is only with the heart that one can see rightly; what is essential is invisible to the eye
-Antoine De Saint-Exupery

Positivity Journal

Today's date:
My positive thought:

○———————————————————————————○

Today's date:
My positive thought:

○———————————————————————————○

Today's date:
My positive thought:

Positivity Journal

Today's date:
My positive thought:

Today's date:
My positive thought:

Today's date:
My positive thought:

Positivity Journal

Today's date:
My positive thought:

○────────────────────────────────────○

Today's date:
My positive thought:

○────────────────────────────────────○

Today's date:
My positive thought:

Never give up.

Positivity Journal

Today's date:
My positive thought:

○———————————————————————————○

Today's date:
My positive thought:

○———————————————————————————○

Today's date:
My positive thought:

Positivity Journal

Today's date:
My positive thought:

Today's date:
My positive thought:

Today's date:
My positive thought:

Positivity Journal

Today's date:
My positive thought:

○────────────────────────────────○

Today's date:
My positive thought:

○────────────────────────────────○

Today's date:
My positive thought:

Find your happy place.

Positivity Journal

Today's date:
My positive thought:

Today's date:
My positive thought:

Today's date:
My positive thought:

Positivity Journal

Today's date:
My positive thought:

○────────────────────────────────────○

Today's date:
My positive thought:

○────────────────────────────────────○

Today's date:
My positive thought:

Positivity Journal

Today's date:
My positive thought:

○———————————————————————○

Today's date:
My positive thought:

○———————————————————————○

Today's date:
My positive thought:

Life is a balance of holding on and letting go-Rumi

Positivity Journal

Today's date:
My positive thought:

○————————————————————————————————○

Today's date:
My positive thought:

○————————————————————————————————○

Today's date:
My positive thought:

Positivity Journal

Today's date:
My positive thought:

○————————————————————————————————○

Today's date:
My positive thought:

○————————————————————————————————○

Today's date:
My positive thought:

Positivity Journal

Today's date:
My positive thought:

○───────────────────────────────○

Today's date:
My positive thought:

○───────────────────────────────○

Today's date:
My postive thought:

Not perfect just forgiven.

Positivity Journal

Today's date:
My positive thought:

○━━━━━━━━━━━━━━━━━━━━━━━━━━━○

Today's date:
My positive thought:

○━━━━━━━━━━━━━━━━━━━━━━━━━━━○

Today's date:
My positive thought:

Positivity Journal

Today's date:
My positive thought:

○————————————————————————○

Today's date:
My positive thought:

○————————————————————————○

Today's date:
My positive thought:

Positivity Journal

Today's date:
My positive thought:

○────────────────────────────○

Today's date:
My positive thought:

○────────────────────────────○

Today's date:
My positive thought:

Do one (secret) good thing today and tell no one.

Positivity Journal

Today's date:
My positive thought:

○————————————————————○

Today's date:
My positive thought:

○————————————————————○

Today's date:
My positive thought:

Positivity Journal

Today's date:
My positive thought:

○———————————————————————○

Today's date:
My positive thought:

○———————————————————————○

Today's date:
My positive thought:

Positivity Journal

Today's date:
My positive thought:

○──○

Today's date:
My positive thought:

○──○

Today's date:
My positive thought:

The best view comes after the hardest climb.

Positivity Journal

Today's date:
My positive thought:

○───────────────────────────○

Today's date:
My positive thought:

○───────────────────────────○

Today's date:
My positive thought:

Positivity Journal

Today's date:
My positive thought:

○────────────────────────────○

Today's date:
My positive thought:

○────────────────────────────○

Today's date:
My positive thought:

Positivity Journal

Today's date:
My positive thought:

O————————————————————————O

Today's date:
My positive thought:

O————————————————————————O

Today's date:
My positive thought:

Believe in yourself.

Positivity Journal

Today's date:
My positive thought:

○────────────────────────────────○

Today's date:
My positive thought:

○────────────────────────────────○

Today's date:
My positive thought:

Positivity Journal

Today's date:
My positive thought:

○───────────────────────────────────○

Today's date:
My positive thought:

○───────────────────────────────────○

Today's date:
My positive thought:

Positivity Journal

Today's date:
My positive thought:

○────────────────────────────────────○

Today's date:
My positive thought:

○────────────────────────────────────○

Today's date:
My positive thought:

Human beings are amazing. If they set their mind, make a plan and never give up, they can accomplish anything.

Positivity Journal

Today's date:
My positive thought:

○───○

Today's date:
My positive thought:

○───○

Today's date:
My positive thought:

Positivity Journal

Today's date:
My positive thought:

○——————————————————————○

Today's date:
My positive thought:

○——————————————————————○

Today's date:
My positive thought:

Positivity Journal

Today's date:
My positive thought:

○———————————————————————————○

Today's date:
My positive thought:

○———————————————————————————○

Today's date:
My positive thought:

The best is yet to come

Positivity Journal

Today's date:
My positive thought:

○────────────────────────────────○

Today's date:
My positive thought:

○────────────────────────────────○

Today's date:
My positive thought:

Positivity Journal

Today's date:
My positive thought:

Today's date:
My positive thought:

Today's date:
My positive thought:

Positivity Journal

Today's date:
My positive thought:

○——○

Today's date:
My positive thought:

○——○

Today's date:
My positive thought:

Trust your crazy ideas.

Positivity Journal

Today's date:
My positive thought:

○───○

Today's date:
My positive thought:

○───○

Today's date:
My positive thought:

Positivity Journal

Today's date:
My positive thought:

○─────────────────────────────────────○

Today's date:
My positive thought:

○─────────────────────────────────────○

Today's date:
My positive thought:

Positivity Journal

Today's date:
My positive thought:

○──○

Today's date:
My positive thought:

○──○

Today's date:
My positive thought:

Follow your dreams they know the way.

Positivity Journal

Today's date:
My positive thought:

○───────────────────────────────○

Today's date:
My positive thought:

○───────────────────────────────○

Today's date:
My positive thought:

Positivity Journal

Today's date:
My positive thought:

○————————————————————○

Today's date:
My positive thought:

○————————————————————○

Today's date:
My positive thought:

Positivity Journal

Today's date:
My positive thought:

○───────────────────────────────────○

Today's date:
My positive thought:

○───────────────────────────────────○

Today's date:
My positive thought:

Enjoy the little things in life, because someday you will look back and realize they were the big things.

Positivity Journal

Today's date:
My positive thought:

○————————————————————————○

Today's date:
My positive thought:

○————————————————————————○

Today's date:
My positive thought:

Positivity Journal

Today's date:
My positive thought:

○────────────────────────────────○

Today's date:
My positive thought:

○────────────────────────────────○

Today's date:
My positive thought:

Positivity Journal

Today's date:
My positive thought:

○―――――――――――――――――――○

Today's date:
My positive thought:

○―――――――――――――――――――○

Today's date:
My positive thought:

You've always had the power my dear, you just had to learn it for yourself.- The Wizard of Oz

Positivity Journal

Today's date:
My positive thought:

○───────────────────────────────○

Today's date:
My positive thought:

○───────────────────────────────○

Today's date:
My positive thought:

Positivity Journal

Today's date:
My positive thought:

Today's date:
My positive thought:

Today's date:
My positive thought:

Positivity Journal

Today's date:
My positive thought:

○————————————————————○

Today's date:
My positive thought:

○————————————————————○

Today's date:
My positive thought:

Will it be easy? Nope. Will it be worth it? Absolutely.

Positivity Journal

Today's date:
My positive thought:

○─────────────────────────────────────○

Today's date:
My positive thought:

○─────────────────────────────────────○

Today's date:
My positive thought:

Positivity Journal

Today's date:
My positive thought:

Today's date:
My positive thought:

Today's date:
My postive thought:

Positivity Journal

Today's date:
My positive thought:

○───○

Today's date:
My positive thought:

○───○

Today's date:
My positive thought:

Believe you can &
you're halfway
there-
T. Roosevelt

Positivity Journal

Today's date:
My positive thought:

Today's date:
My positive thought:

Today's date:
My positive thought:

Positivity Journal

Today's date:
My positive thought:

Today's date:
My positive thought:

Today's date:
My positive thought:

Positivity Journal

Today's date:
My positive thought:

○——○

Today's date:
My positive thought:

○——○

Today's date:
My positive thought:

Take the risk or
lose the chance.

Positivity Journal

Today's date:
My positive thought:

○────────────────────────────────────○

Today's date:
My positive thought:

○────────────────────────────────────○

Today's date:
My positive thought:

Positivity Journal

Today's date:
My positive thought:

○─────────────────────────────○

Today's date:
My positive thought:

○─────────────────────────────○

Today's date:
My positive thought:

Positivity Journal

Today's date:
My positive thought:

○━━━━━━━━━━━━━━━━━━━━━━━━━━○

Today's date:
My positive thought:

○━━━━━━━━━━━━━━━━━━━━━━━━━━○

Today's date:
My positive thought:

The trouble is, you think you have time.

Positivity Journal

Today's date:
My positive thought:

○─────────────────────────────────────○

Today's date:
My positive thought:

○─────────────────────────────────────○

Today's date:
My positive thought:

Positivity Journal

Today's date:
My positive thought:

○─────────────────────────────────────○

Today's date:
My positive thought:

○─────────────────────────────────────○

Today's date:
My positive thought:

Positivity Journal

Today's date:
My positive thought:

○────────────────────────────────────○

Today's date:
My positive thought:

○────────────────────────────────────○

Today's date:
My positive thought:

Every saint has a past and every sinner a future-
Oscar Wilde

Positivity Journal

Today's date:
My positive thought:

Today's date:
My positive thought:

Today's date:
My positive thought:

Positivity Journal

Today's date:
My positive thought:

○─────────────────────────────────────○

Today's date:
My positive thought:

○─────────────────────────────────────○

Today's date:
My positive thought:

Positivity Journal

Today's date:
My positive thought:

○————————————————————————————————○

Today's date:
My positive thought:

○————————————————————————————————○

Today's date:
My positive thought:

Storms don't last forever.

Positivity Journal

Today's date:
My positive thought:

Today's date:
My positive thought:

Today's date:
My positive thought:

Positivity Journal

Today's date:
My positive thought:

Today's date:
My positive thought:

Today's date:
My positive thought:

Positivity Journal

Today's date:
My positive thought:

○────────────────────────────────────○

Today's date:
My positive thought:

○────────────────────────────────────○

Today's date:
My positive thought:

There are so many
beautiful reasons
to be happy.

Positivity Journal

Today's date:
My positive thought:

Today's date:
My positive thought:

Today's date:
My positive thought:

Positivity Journal

Today's date:
My positive thought:

Today's date:
My positive thought:

Today's date:
My postive thought:

Positivity Journal

Today's date:
My positive thought:

○────────────────────────────────○

Today's date:
My positive thought:

○────────────────────────────────○

Today's date:
My positive thought:

When life gets
blurry adjust your
focus.

Positivity Journal

Today's date:
My positive thought:

Today's date:
My positive thought:

Today's date:
My positive thought:

Positivity Journal

Today's date:
My positive thought:

○───○

Today's date:
My positive thought:

○───○

Today's date:
My positive thought:

Positivity Journal

Today's date:
My positive thought:

○━━━━━━━━━━━━━━━━━━━━━━━━━━○

Today's date:
My positive thought:

○━━━━━━━━━━━━━━━━━━━━━━━━━━○

Today's date:
My positive thought:

Don't count the days. Make the days count.

Positivity Journal

Today's date:
My positive thought:

○————————————————————————————————————○

Today's date:
My positive thought:

○————————————————————————————————————○

Today's date:
My positive thought:

Positivity Journal

Today's date:
My positive thought:

○──○

Today's date:
My positive thought:

○──○

Today's date:
My positive thought:

Positivity Journal

Today's date:
My positive thought:

○────────────────────────────────────○

Today's date:
My positive thought:

○────────────────────────────────────○

Today's date:
My positive thought:

Enjoy the journey.

Positivity Journal

Today's date:
My positive thought:

○────────────────────────────────○

Today's date:
My positive thought:

○────────────────────────────────○

Today's date:
My positve thought:

Positivity Journal

Today's date:
My positive thought:

○──○

Today's date:
My positive thought:

○──○

Today's date:
My postive thought:

Positivity Journal

Today's date:
My positive thought:

○———————————————————————○

Today's date:
My positive thought:

○———————————————————————○

Today's date:
My postive thought:

Positivity Journal

Today's date:
My positive thought:

○————————————————————————————————○

Today's date:
My positive thought:

○————————————————————————————————○

Today's date:
My positive thought:

Positivity Journal

Today's date:
My positive thought:

○——————————————————————○

Today's date:
My positive thought:

○——————————————————————○

Today's date:
My positive thought:

Stay humble, work hard and be kind.

Positivity Journal

Today's date:
My positive thought:

○————————————————————————○

Today's date:
My positive thought:

○————————————————————————○

Today's date:
My positive thought:

Positivity Journal

Today's date:
My positive thought:

Today's date:
My positive thought:

Today's date:
My positive thought:

Positivity Journal

Today's date:
My positive thought:

○────────────────────────────────────○

Today's date:
My positive thought:

○────────────────────────────────────○

Today's date:
My positive thought:

It's free to be kind.

Positivity Journal

Today's date:
My positive thought:

○────────────────────────────────────○

Today's date:
My positive thought:

○────────────────────────────────────○

Today's date:
My positive thought:

Positivity Journal

Today's date:
My positive thought:

Today's date:
My positive thought:

Today's date:
My positive thought:

Positivity Journal

Today's date:
My positive thought:

○────────────────────────────────────○

Today's date:
My positive thought:

○────────────────────────────────────○

Today's date:
My positive thought:

Nothing is permanent in this wicked world, not even our troubles.- Charlie Chaplin

Positivity Journal

Today's date:
My positive thought:

○─────────────────────────────────────○

Today's date:
My positive thought:

○─────────────────────────────────────○

Today's date:
My positive thought:

Positivity Journal

Today's date:
My positive thought:

Today's date:
My positive thought:

Today's date:
My positive thought:

Positivity Journal

Today's date:
My positive thought:

○────────────────────────────────○

Today's date:
My positive thought:

○────────────────────────────────○

Today's date:
My positive thought:

Positivity Journal

Today's date:
My positive thought:

○————————————————————————————○

Today's date:
My positive thought:

○————————————————————————————○

Today's date:
My positive thought:

Other Books With Soul:
Words I want to Say
Every Breath- A Journal of Gratitude & Blessings
Crazy Ramblings of a Pregnant Woman
Remember When: Guest Book
Camp Memories
Reflections from the Beach
The Plan
The Adventures of US
Reflections of My Year
Pregnancy Journal: When We Were One

Anniversary editions available on Amazon:
1st Anniversary: One Epic Year
5th Anniversary: Five Epic Years
10th Anniversary: Ten Epic Years
15th Anniversary: Fifteen Epic Years
20th Anniversary: Twenty Epic Years
25th Anniversary: Twenty-five Epic Years
30th Anniversary: Thirty Epic Years
35th Anniversary: Thirty-five Epic Years
40th Anniversary: Forty Epic Years
45th Anniversary: Forty-five Epic Years
50th Anniversary: Fifty Epic Years

Perfect Anniversary Gift

Books With Soul

Books with Soul believes in sharing gifts that inspire and motivate others to create memories and keep a record of the story of their life.

What if... you had a record of your memories or someone you loved?

INSPIRATION COMES IN ALL SIZES, SHAPES & IDEAS

WE believe every life is worth a few written words to pass on or reflect on in the future. You don't have to be an author to tell the story of your life. Just be you. Today will someday be the good old days, remember them.

Books with Soul offers inspirational journals with questions & thoughts to help record memories for the most novice of journalers. Birthday, milestones, wedding and baby gifts. Help someone write their life story.

Questions? Email info@bookswithsoul.com
We appreciate every reader, every traveler and recorder of history. We would love if you took the time to write a review on Amazon and let us know if the books motivated you.

Find more journals, inspiration, diaries, coloring books and gifts for every milestone at:
www.bookswithsoul.com

If you would like to have a personalized journal for an organization, company, group, club, or activity, contact Books with Soul. Special unique journals in 25 quantities or more can be created.

*if someone bought you this journal, pay it forward and
buy a journal
for someone you care about.
Help them become more positive in life, love and family.

Thank you!
If this make you even a little bit more positive, **please leave a review on Amazon!** Let's help the world become more positive. Imagine if everyone did this every morning!

Sign up for our newsletter on sales and giveaways from Bookswithsoul.com

Books with Soul ™

was inspired from a lover of music and life, who believed in the soul. He had a collection of wonderful things. Physical memories you could read, touch, and listen to- including thousands of vinyl albums.

Old school music, that lasts forever. In 2018, he passed away from brain cancer, but his memory lives on as others go old school. Collect pieces of your history, put pencil to paper, and record written memories.

A physical book will not be lost in the cloud and will last longer than a lifetime.

Keep a record of the story of your life. Your Words. Your Pages.

This is for you Mark.

Thanks for taking the time to write one positive thought each day.

Keep this book somewhere safe.

Hide it, share it or leave it for someone you love.
START A YEARLY COLLECTION.

OR

GIFT ONE AS A SPECIAL GIFT

A VARIETY OF JOURNALS EXIST: TRY ONE

WITH DAILY INSPIRATIONAL QUOTES,

OR WRITING PROMPTS TO KEEP YOU

WRITING.

VISIT THE WEBSITE FOR SALES & SWAG

Made in the USA
San Bernardino, CA
23 January 2019